Blueprint ONE

GRAMMAR PRACTICE

Pat Mugglestone

Longman Group UK Limited
Longman House, Burnt Mill, Harlow,
Essex CM20 2JE, England
and Associated Companies throughout the world.

First published 1993

Set in Adobe PostScript Concorde 10 on 12pt
Printed by Scotprint, Musselburgh, Scotland

ISBN 0 582 09111 X

Acknowledgements

Illustrated by Phil Bannister, Lorraine Harrison, Pauline Hazelwood,
Chris Pavely, Taurus Graphics

We are grateful to the following for permission to reproduce copyright
photographs:

The J Allan Cash Photolibrary for pages 21 (bottom) and 22; Life File
Photographic Library for page 21 (top); Tony Stone Worldwide for pages 31
and 62 (bottom); Telegraph Colour Library for page 62 (top); Viewfinder
Colour Library for page 49.

CONTENTS

UNITS 1–5

House: Sea View

Boat: Victory

Dog: Blackie

Margaret Sampson = William Sampson

Thomas   Kirsten   Matthew

Verb: *to be*

Full form	Short form
I am	I'm
You are	You're
He/She/It is	He/She/It's

1 Look at the family tree and complete the sentences using short forms.

1 I ..'m.. Matthew.

2 I ..'m.. called Matt for short.

3 She ..is.. my sister.

4 His name ..is.. Thomas.

5 I ..'s.. his brother.

6 You .... a good dog, Blackie.

7 You ..are.. my friend.

Subject pronouns and possessive adjectives

Subject pronoun	Possessive adjective
I	my
you	your
he	his
she	her
it	its

2 Write sentences about the Sampson family, using full forms and possessive adjectives.

1 (she/Kirsten)
Her name is Kirsten.

2 (he/William)
his names William

3 (you/Thomas)
your names Thomas

4 (she/Margaret)
she names Margaret

5 (I/Matthew)
My Matthew

4

3 Match the names and write sentences. Use short forms.

1	Matthew	Kirsty
2	William	Tom
3	Margaret	Matt
4	Kirsten	Will
5	Thomas	Maggie

1 *His name's Matthew but he's called Matt for short.*
2 *His name's William but he's called Will for short*
3 *Her names Margaret but she's called Maggie for short*
4 *Her names Kirsten but she's called Kirsty for short*
5 *His names Thomas but he's called Tom for short*

Names of people and things

> What's (his) name?
> (His) name's (Thomas).
>
> What's the name of (the boat)?
> It's called (Victory).

4 Write questions for these answers.

1 *What's her name?*
  Her name's Kirsten.
2 *What's the name of the dog?*
  It's called Blackie.
3 *What's the name of the...*
  It's called Victory.
4 *What's the name of Son (Father)*
  His name's William.
5 *What's the name of mother*
  Her name's Margaret.
6 *What's name of house*
  It's called Sea View.
7 *What has*
  My name's Matthew.

Genitive s

> my father's name
> my parents' name

5 Write the correct form of the genitive.

1 His sisters name is Kirsten.
  sister's name.
2 Matt and Tom are boys names.
3 What's his mothers name?
4 His parents boat is called Victory.
5 What's your partners name?
6 What's Matthews dog called?

6 Is or gentive 's? Write the full form of the verb where appropriate.

1 My father's name is William.
  ——
2 What's the name of the house?
  What is
3 Maggie is a girl's name.
4 His dog's called Blackie.
5 My name's Matt.
6 Is he Matt's brother?
7 What's William called for short?

UNIT 2

Greetings and goodbyes

7 Match the two parts of the conversations.

a) Night.   e) How do you do.
b) Bye.   f) Thanks. And the same to you.
c) Hello.   g) Good morning.
d) Yes, O.K.

1 Hi.
  c) Hello.

2 How do you do.
  e) How do you do

3 Goodbye.
  Bye

4 Have a nice weekend.
  Thanks. And the same to you

5 Goodnight.
  night

6 Good morning.
  Good morning

7 See you on Monday.
  Yes, O.K

Question words

8 Complete the questions, using the correct question words.

What	Who	How

1 *What* 's your name?
It's Thomas.

2 *Who* 's that?
It's Mr Sampson.

3 *What* 's that?
It's my English textbook.

4 *How* are you?
Fine, thanks.

5 *What* day is it today?
It's Monday.

6 How do you do!
How do you do!

7 *How* is your brother?
He's O.K.

8 *Who* is Lynn?
She's my friend.

9 *What* is Pierre's name in English?
It's Peter.

10 *What* 's your mother's name?
Margaret.

Punctuation

9 Rewrite the conversation using the correct punctuation. Use the following marks:

full stop (.) question mark (?)
apostrophe(') CAPITAL letter

ANN: hello tom how are you
  Hello, Tom. How are you?

TOM: im fine thanks what day is it today

ANN: its friday its my fathers birthday today and its my mothers birthday on sunday.

TOM: and its my birthday on monday.

UNIT 3

Verb: *to be* (Present simple)

Positive	Negative	Question	Short answers				
I'm French.	I'm not English.	Am I French?	Yes,	I am.	No,	I'm not.
She's English.	She isn't Spanish.	Is she English?		she is.		she isn't.
They're Italian.	They aren't French.	Are they Italian?		they are.		they aren't.

10 Write statements and questions, using the following nationalities and cities.

| Italian | Tokyo | Moscow | Paris | Algiers | Madrid | English | Portuguese |

1 *I'm English.*
....
Are you from London?

2 They're Russian.
Are they from Moscow?.................

3 He's Japanese.
....

4 We're French.
....

5 ....
Are they from Rome?

6 ....
Is she from Lisbon?

7 I'm Spanish.
....

8 They're Algerian.
....

11 Answer the questions.

1 Is he French?
No, he isn't. He's.............. American.

2 Are they Swedish?
No they isnt They............German.

3 Is Kyoto in China?
No he doesnt Hes.............in Japan.

4 Are you Dutch?
..............I..............German.

5 Am I in England?
..............you..............in Wales.

6 Are we in Spain?
..............in Portugal.

7 Is Buenos Aires in Brazil?
..............in Argentina.

8 Are you in France?
..............I..............in Spain.

12 Rewrite the paragraph, using short forms.

I am Karen. I am American and I am from New York. My father is from Boston. His name is Richard but he is called Dick for short. My mother is not American. She is German. She is from Cologne. My parents and I are not in the USA this week. We are in Germany.

I'm Karen. I'm American and I'm from New York. My father is from Boston. His name Richard but he's called Dick for short. My mother's is not American. She's German. She's from Cologne. My parents and I'm not in USA this week. We are in Germany.

7

UNIT 4

Articles

	Indefinite article	**Definite article**
Singular	a table an orange	the table the orange
Plural	tables oranges	(the) tables (the) oranges

13 **Complete the dialogue, using *a*, *an* or *the*.**

SUE: Where are my pens?

BEN: They're on [1] _the_ table.

SUE: What's that?

BEN: It's [2] .... letter from Maria.
There's [3] .... Italian stamp on [4] .... envelope. What's that in your bag?

SUE: It's [5] .... book.

BEN: Is it [6] .... notebook?

SUE: No. It's [7] .... address book.

BEN: Where are my keys?

SUE: They're in [8] .... bag, too.

Demonstrative pronouns

Singular	**Plural**
this that	these those

14 **Write questions and answers, using *this*, *that*, *these* or *those*.**

1 *What's this?*
It's a table.

2 ....
....

3 ....
....

4 ....
....

5 *What are those?*
They're ....

6 ....
....

7 ....
....

8 ....
....

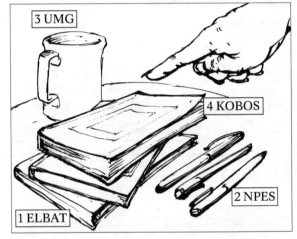

3 UMG
4 KOBOS
2 NPES
1 ELBAT

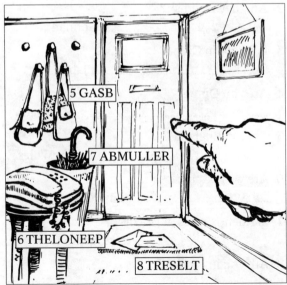

5 GASB
7 ABMULLER
6 THELONEEP
8 TRESELT

Prepositions of place

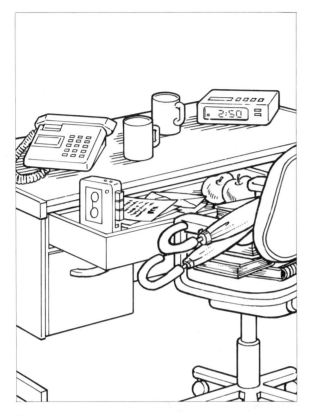

15 Write questions with *Where* and answers using *in* or *on*.

1 Where is the telephone?
   It's on the desk.

2 *Where are the books*?
   They're on the chair.

3 ....
   It's in the drawer.

4 Where are the umbrellas?
   ....

5 Where are the letters?
   ....

6 Where is the clock?
   ....

7 ....
   They're on the desk.

8 ....
   They're in the drawer.

Personal information

16 Look at the boxes and complete the conversation with the correct questions.

What	is ('s)	your	address surname telephone number	?
	are		first names	

How do you spell it?

Are you	English married	?

How old are you?

Where are you from?

1 A: *What's your surname?*
   B: Heyden.

2 A: ....
   B: H E Y D E N.

3 A: ....
   B: Michael Stephen.

4 A: ....
   B: Twenty-three.

5 A: ....
   B: No, I'm not. I'm Welsh.

6 A: ....
   B: Cardiff.

7 A: ....
   B: 3, Church Road, Cardiff CF4 7BJ

8 A: ....
   B: 0222 553687
   A: Thank you.

CHECK UNITS 1–5

Choose the correct answer

1 Circle the correct answer.

1 What *is*/*are* your name?

2 My *mothers'*/*mother's* name is Susan.

3 The *textbook's name is*/*textbook is called* Blueprint One.

4 This is my boat. *Its*/*It's* called Victory.

5 A: How are you?
B: *Fine, thanks*/*How do you do*.

6 A: Good evening, Mr Jones.
B: *Goodnight*/*Good evening*, Mrs Short.

7 A: *Who*/*How* is this?
B: It's my brother.

8 *He called*/*He's called* Dick for short.

9 A: Is she British?
B: No, she *isn't*/*aren't*.

10 A: Where's the lamp?
B: It's *in*/*on* the table.

11 A: What's that?
B: It's *an*/*a* envelope.

12 A: What are *this*/*these*?
B: They're pencils.

13 A: What colour is *a*/*the* pen?
B: It's black.

14 A: *What's*/*How's* this in English?
B: It's a wallet.

15 A: What's your telephone number?
B: *It's*/*That's* 071–865–6598

16 Where's *you*/*your* sister?

17 Where *is*/*are* the pens?

18 Is he *French*/*France*?

19 A: Are you eighteen?
B: Yes, *I am*/*I'm not*.

20 Where *you are*/*are you* from?

Correct the mistakes

2 There is one mistake underlined in each sentence. Note the mistakes and then write correct sentences.

1 Margareta is Margaret on English.
Margareta is Margaret in English.

2 Linda is a girl name.
....

3 A: What's the name of your house?
B: It's name is The Cedars.
....

4 This is my mother. His name is Mary.
....

5 How you spell your name?
....

Complete the conversation

3 Complete the conversation with the correct words.

MATTHEW: Hi. 1 *What's* your name?

LINDA: 2 I .... Linda. And you?

MATTHEW: 3 .... name's Matthew, but 4.................... called Matt for short.

LINDA: 5 .... that?

MATTHEW: 6 .... my brother. 7 .... name's Thomas. Are you 8 .... America?

LINDA: Yes, I 9 .... I'm 10 .... Boston.

> **CHECK YOUR PROGRESS**
> Look back at your answers for Units 1–5.
> Note your problem exercises and revise them.

UNITS 6–10

Modal: *can* (ability)

Positive	Negative
I can swim.	I can't (cannot) swim.

Question
Can you swim?

Short answers	
Yes, I can.	No, I can't.

1 Write sentences, using *can/can't*.

1 (Tessa/ski/✓)
She can ski.

2 (Andy/Paul/ski/✗)
They can't ski.

3 (Paul/play table tennis/✗)
....

4 (Tessa/windsurf/✗)
....

5 (Andy/play football/✓)
....

6 (Andy/Tessa/swim/✓)
....

7 (Paul/play tennis/✓)
....

8 (Tessa/play football/✗)
....

2 Write questions and short answers, using *can*.

1 (windsurf)
.......*Can* you *windsurf*...........?

No, *I can't.*...........

2 (play football)
.... Paul and Andy ....
Yes, they ....

3 (play table tennis)
.... you and Andy ....
....
Yes, we ....

4 (ski)
.... you ....
Yes, ...

5 (play tennis)
.... Paul ....
Yes, ...

6 (ski)
.... Andy and Paul ....
No, ...

7 (swim)
.... you and Paul ....
Yes, ...

8 (windsurf)
.... Andy ....
No, ...

	(swim)	(ski)	(windsurf)	(tennis)	(table tennis)	(football)
ANDY	3	0	0	0	2	3
TESSA	3	1	0	0	2	0
PAUL	2	0	1	3	0	2

0	= not at all	2	= quite well
1	= a little	3	= very well

Adverbs of degree and modifiers

3 Look at the table and write sentences, using *can* and the correct adverb of degree.

1 (Andy/ski)
Andy can't ski at all.

2 (Tessa/ski)
....

3 (Andy and Tessa/play table tennis)
....
....

4 (Paul/play tennis)
....

5 (Tessa/play tennis)
....

6 (Paul/windsurf)
....

7 (Andy and Tessa/windsurf)
....
....

And/but/or

4 Complete the sentences, using *and*, *but* or *or*.

1

Paul Dobson: Paul can swim quite well [1] **and** he can play football quite well, too, [2] _____ he can't ski [3] _____ play table tennis.

2

Tessa Goodwin: Tessa can swim very well [4] _____ she can play table tennis quite well, too, [5] _____ she can't play tennis [6] _____ waterski.

3

Andy Smith: Andy can swim [7] _____ play football very well. He can't play tennis, [8] _____ he can play table tennis quite well. He can't ski [9] _____ waterski.

Verb: *have got*

Positive	
I've	got a sister.
He's	

Negative	
I haven't	got a sister.
He hasn't	

Question	
Have you	got any sisters?
Has he	

Short answers				
Yes,	I have.	No,	I haven't.
	he has.		he hasn't.

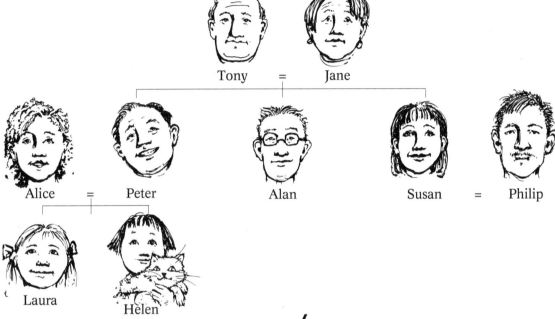

Tony = Jane

Alice = Peter   Alan   Susan = Philip

Laura   Helen

5 Complete the sentences with the correct form of *have got.*

JANE: "¹ *I've got* two sons and a daughter. My son, Peter, and his wife, Alice, ² .... two daughters. I ³ .... any grandsons. My daughter, Susan, ⁴ .... any children."

SUSAN: "⁵ I .... two brothers but I ⁶ .... any sisters. Philip and I ⁷ .... any children. My brother Peter ⁸ .... two children."

HELEN: "⁹ .... a sister but I ¹⁰ .... any brothers. ¹¹ I .... a white cat but my sister ¹² .... a cat or a dog."

6 Write Peter's short answers.

1 Have you got a sister?
   Yes, I have. ....

2 Has your sister got any children?
    ....

3 Have your parents got any grandchildren?
    ....

4 Have you and Alice got any children?
    ....

5 Have you and Alice got any sons?
    ....

6 Has Helen got a white cat?
    ....

7 Have your children got any uncles?
    ....

Question words: *How many*

7 **Write questions and answers using the correct form of *have got*.**

1 (children/Alan)
How many children has Alan got?
He hasn't got any.

2 (brothers/Susan)
....
....

3 (children/Jane and Tony)
....
....

4 (sisters/Helen)
....
....

5 (brothers/Helen)
....
....

6 (nieces/Susan)
....
....

7 (children/Susan and Philip)
....
....

Short forms

8 **Rewrite the paragraph using short forms.**

My name is Alan. I am from England. My parents, Jane and Tony Walker have got three children and two grandchildren. I have got one brother, Peter, and he has got two daughters. Helen has got a white cat. It is called Snowy. My sister, Susan, has not got any children and I have not got any children.

My name's Alan.
....
....
....
....
....
....
....
....
....
....
....

Verb: *to be* (Past simple)

She was	American.
They were	

9 **Match the names and nationalities. Then write sentences, using *was* or *were*.**

1 John F. Kennedy — a) Egyptian
2 Leonardo da Vinci and Michelangelo — b) American
3 Saint Joan of Arc — c) English
4 Cleopatra — d) Spanish
5 Goya and Picasso — e) Italian
6 The Brontë sisters, Charlotte, Emily and Anne — f) Austrian
7 Wolfgang Amadeus Mozart — g) French

1 *b) John F. Kennedy was American.*
....
2 ....
....
3 ....
....
4 ....
....
5 ....
....
6 ....
....
7 ....
....

UNIT 8

Present simple

Question				Positive			Negative		
Where	do	you they	live?	I They	live	in London.	I They	don't	live in Oxford.
	does	she		She	lives		She	doesn't	

Question			Short answers						
Do	you they	live in south London?	Yes,	I they	do.	No,	I they	don't.
Does	she			she	does.		she	doesn't.

10 **Write questions, using the present simple.**

1 (Where/you/come from)
Where do you come from?
I come from Scotland.

2 (Where/you/live)
....
In Glasgow.

3 (What/you/do)
....
I teach music.

4 (Where/you/work)
....
In a school near Glasgow.

5 (What/your father/do)
....
He works for the government.

6 (What/your mother/do)
....
She's a journalist.

7 (Where/they/live)
....
In London.

11 **Look at the information in Exercise 10. Complete the sentences, using the present simple.**

REPORT ON MS DOROTHY PECK
She (come) [1] ...*comes*... from
Scotland and she (live)
[2] .... in Glasgow. She
(not live) [3] .... with
her parents. They (live)
[4] .... in London. Her
father (work) [5] .... for
the government. She (teach)
[6] .... music. She (not
work) [7] .... in the
centre of Glasgow, but she
(work) [8] .... in a big
school near the city.

UNIT 9

Like + -ing

Positive	
I like	dancing.
She likes	

Negative	
I don't	like dancing.
She doesn't	

Question	
Do you	like dancing?
Does she	

Short answers			
Yes,	I do.	No,	I don't.
	she does.		she doesn't.

12 Write questions and answers.

1 (he/ 🏊) *Does he like swimming* ?
Yes, *he does.*
....

2 (you/ 🎿) ....
No, I ....

3 (they/ 🏄) ....
Yes, ...

4 (she/ 🎾) ....
Yes, ...

5 (he/ 💃) ....
No, ...

6 (they/ 🎤) ....
No, ...

Subject and object pronouns

Subject pronouns	Object pronouns
I	me
you	you
he	him
she	her
it	it
we	us
they	them

13 Answer the questions, using the correct form of *love*, *like* or *hate*.

1 Do you and your friend like singing? (hate)
No, we hate it. ....

2 Do you enjoy dancing? (like/very much)
....

3 Does your mother like children? (love)
....

4 Does your father like dogs?
(not/like/very much)
....

5 Do you and your brother like Cher?
(like/very much)
....

6 Do your parents like cities? (hate)
....

7 Does your cat love you? (love)
....

UNIT 10

Prepositions of place

14 Complete the paragraph with the correct prepositions.

in (x4)   on (x2)   near (x2)

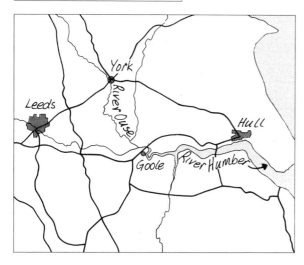

"I live ¹...*in*... Goole, a town ².......... the north of England. Goole is ³.......... the River Ouse ⁴.......... the east coast. I enjoy living ⁵.......... the sea. I live ⁶.......... a house ⁷.......... the centre of the town. Goole is ⁸.......... three big cities – Hull, Leeds and York."

What's it like?

16 Match the two parts and write questions and answers.

1 Rome — a very boring man

2 the factory — an ugly, modern building

3 your uncle → a beautiful, historical city

4 your town — an interesting woman

5 his sister — a big, modern flat

6 their home — a small, interesting place

Articles

15 Write the sentences using *a/an* or *the* and capital letters where necessary.

1 they live in .... town on .... east coast of scotland.
   They live in a town on the east coast of Scotland.

2 jan comes from france but her husband comes from .... united states.
   ....
   ....

3 I live in .... old house in .... country in .... centre of england.
   ....
   ....

4 los angeles is in .... west of .... united states on .... pacific coast.
   ....
   ....

5 chris is .... boy's name and .... girl's name in english.
   ....
   ....

6 .... eiffel tower is in paris.
   ....
   ....

1 *What's Rome like?*
   It's a beautiful, historical city.

2 ....
   ....

3 ....
   ....

4 ....
   ....

5 ....
   ....

6 ....
   ....

17

CHECK UNITS 6–10

Choose the correct answer

1 Circle the correct answer.

1 A: Do you like music?
   B: Yes, I *like/(do)*.

2 She can *swims/swim*.

3 How many brothers *you have got/have you got*?

4 I live *in/on* the centre of the town.

5 Do they like *sing/singing*?

6 I haven't *got/get* a dog.

7 She can *very well dance/dance very well*.

8 I *can dance not/can't dance* at all.

9 He *have/has* got a big flat.

10 I can play tennis *a little/little*.

11 Does she *live/lives* in Oxford?

12 My grandparents *was/were* Welsh.

13 We don't like *them/they*.

14 They live *on/at* the south coast.

15 They enjoy playing *the football/football*.

16 She can't dance or *sing/can't sing*.

17 I haven't got *the/any* sisters.

18 London is *on/in* the river Thames.

19 He *doesn't/don't* live with his parents.

20 A: What do you do?
    B: I'm *student/a student*.

Correct the mistakes

2 There is one mistake underlined in each sentence. Note the mistakes and then write correct sentences.

1 He comes from <u>United States</u>.
   He comes from the United States.

2 A: Has he got any children?
   B: Yes, he's <u>got</u>.
   ....

3 I <u>like very much music</u>.
   ....

4 They can swim <u>and</u> they can't ski.
   ....

5 Where <u>you come</u> from?
   ....

Complete the conversation

3 Complete the conversation with the correct words.

A: How old [1].....*are*..... you?

B: I'm nineteen [2].................. old.

A: Where [3].................. you live?

B: I live [4].................. a small flat [5]..................
    Oxford.

A: What is Oxford [6].................. ?

B: It's [7].................. beautiful old city, famous
    [8].................. its university.

A: Have you got [9].................. brothers or sisters?

B: I've got two sisters but I [10].................. got any
    brothers.

> **CHECK YOUR PROGRESS**
> Look back at your answers for Units 6–10.
> Note your problem exercises and revise them.

UNITS 11–15

UNIT 11

Present simple

1 Look at the information, then write questions and answers, using: *What time...?*

1 (disco/open)
What time does the disco open?
It opens at seven o'clock in the evening.

2 (pizzeria/close)
....
....
....

3 (coffee shops/open)
....
....
....

4 (swimming pools/open)
....
....
....

5 (disco/close)
....
....
....

6 (coffee shops/close)
....
....
....

Prepositions of time

2 Complete the sentences with the correct preposition:

at(x7)	on(x2)	in(x5)	from(x2)	to(x2)

1 The pizzeria opens ....at.... 10 o'clock .... the morning.

2 The restaurant opens .... noon. It closes .... 3 p.m. .... 6 p.m. .... the afternoon. It opens .... the evening and closes .... midnight.

3 The restaurant is closed .... Monday and the disco is closed .... Sunday.

4 The swimming pools open .... the morning .... 7 o'clock.

5 The disco is open .... night. It closes .... 2 a.m.

6 The coffee shops are open .... 9 a.m. .... 5.30 p.m. They are not open .... the evening or .... night.

Everything is here in your holiday village

Three coffee shops
Open: 09.00 – 17.30 every day

A restaurant
Open: 12.00 – 15.00/18.00 – 24.00
Closed: Monday

A pizzeria
Open: 10.00 – 23.00 every day

A disco
Open: 19.00 – 02.00
Closed: Sunday

Two swimming pools
Open: 07.00 – 22.00

UNIT 12

Zero article

I go	to	school bed	at 8 o'clock.
		home	

I go	to	the bank the station	at 8 o'clock.

3 Complete the sentences with an article
(*a/the*) or no article.

Nick is [1].....*a*.... student, but in [2]............ evenings
he is [3]............waiter. He goes to [4]............ work at
5 p.m. and has [5]............. dinner before he starts
[6]........... work at 6 p.m. He finishes [7]........... work
at midnight. Then he goes [8]........... home. He
usually has [9]............ shower and then goes to
[10]............ bed.

Adverbs of frequency

4 Look at the information and make sentences about what Nick does on Sunday,
using the correct adverb of frequency.

		never	sometimes	often	usually	always
1	study in the library	✓				
2	sleep all day		✓			
3	have a big dinner					✓
4	am at the restaurant	✓				
5	go out with my friends in the evening				✓	
6	telephone my parents			✓		
7	go for a walk		✓			
8	am in bed before midnight					✓

1 *He never studies in the library on Sunday.* ....

2 ....

3 ....

4 ....

5 ....

6 ....

7 ....

8 ....

UNIT 13

Preposition *by* and means of transport

| I go by bus/car/boat/train. |
| I walk/drive/cycle. |

5 Look at the information and answer the questions.

1

usually   sometimes   never

A: How do you go to school?

B: *I usually walk. I sometimes cycle. I never go by bus.*

2

often   sometimes   never

A: How does your sister go to work?

B: She ....

....

3

usually   sometimes   never

A: How do Mr and Mrs Grey travel when they go on holiday?

B: They ....

....

What? How? How far? How long?

6 Look at the information and write conversations.

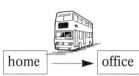

home → office

(secretaries)   3 miles/15 minutes

1 A: What do they do?

B: *They're secretaries.*

A: How do they get from their home to work?

B: *By* ....

A: How far is it?

B: ....

A: How long does it take?

B: ....

flat → hospital

(doctor)   10 miles/30 minutes

2 A: What does she do?

B: ....

A: ....

.... ?

B: ....

A: .... ?

B: ....

A: .... ?

B: ....

Because

7 Match the answers to the questions. Then write answers, using *because.*

1 Why doesn't he drive to work?

2 Why is the bank closed?

3 Why does she like San Diego?

4 Why does he live in the country?

5 Why is he called George in English?

6 Why does she start work at 9.30 p.m. and finish at 8 a.m.?

7 Why doesn't he fly to Paris?

a) is Sunday

b) doesn't like towns and cities

c) his name's Jorge

d) hasn't got a car

e) never travels by plane

f) has a big harbour and beautiful beaches

g) is on night duty at the hospital

1 *d) He doesn't drive to work because he hasn't got a car.*

2 ....

3 ....

4 ....

5 ....

6 ....

7 ....

UNIT 14

There is/there are

Positive	Negative
There's a chair.	There isn't a chair.
There are two chairs.	There aren't any chairs.

8 Look at the hotel room. Write sentences about the things in the brackets ( ).

1 (television) *There isn't a television.*

2 (beds) *There are two beds.*

3 (table) ....

4 (pictures) ....

5 (windows) ....

6 (wardrobe) ....

7 (lamps) ....

8 (clock) ....

9 (telephone) ....

Question	Short answers				
Is there a chair?	Yes,	there is.	No,	there isn't.	
Are there any chairs?		there are.		there aren't.	

9 Look at the hotel room again. Write questions and answers.

1 *Is there an armchair? Yes, there is.*

4  ....

2 ....

5  ....

3  ....

6  ....

Short answers

10 Complete the dialogues, using short answers.

A: Excuse me, are there any small hotels here?

B: Yes, ¹ *there are*...................................

A: Is there is a good small hotel in the centre of town?

B: Yes, ² .... It's called The Cavendish.

A: Is there a restaurant in the hotel?

B: Yes, ³ .... It's very good.

A: Is the restaurant open on Sunday?

B: No, I'm afraid ⁴ ....

A: Have all the rooms got a telephone?

B: No, ⁵ ....

A: Have all the rooms got a television?

B: Yes, ⁶ ....

UNIT 15

Present continuous

Positive	
I'm	reading a book.
She's	
They're	

Negative	
I'm not	reading a book.
She isn't	
They aren't	

Question	
Are you	reading a book?
Is she	
Are they	

Short answers				
Yes,	I am.	No,	I'm not.
	she is.		she isn't.
	they are.		they aren't.

11 Look at the pictures and write sentences using the present continuous. Choose the correct verb and object from the boxes below.

make	buy	go
write	play	read
have	watch	

football	bed	letter
lunch	newspaper	
book	cake	television

1  *I'm writing a letter.*

2  *We*

3

4

5

6

7

8

12 Look at the pictures in Exercise 11 again and write questions and answers, using the present continuous.

1 *What is she doing?*
  She's writing a letter

2 .... *they*

3 ....

4 ....

5 ....

6 ....

7 ....

8 ....

CHECK *UNITS 11–15*

Choose the correct answer

1 Circle the correct answer.

1 I get up *at/on* seven o'clock.
2 What time does the shop *open/opens*?
3 They're going *bed/to bed*.
4 *I write/I'm writing* this postcard in the park.
5 They sometimes work *in/at* night.
6 There *are/is* two pens on the desk.
7 I usually drink tea *in/on* the morning.
8 We have *the lunch/lunch* at 12.30.
9 She never drives to *work/the work*.
10 They *often are/are often* asleep before midnight.
11 He is *doctor/a doctor*.
12 Why *isn't/not* the bank open?
13 A: Do they like tennis?
   B: Yes, they *like/do*.
14 There aren't *the/any* hotels here.
15 She *reading/is reading* a book at the moment.
16 A: What *you are/are you* writing?
   B: A letter.
17 Are there *any/the* armchairs in the room?
18 A: Is there a letter on the table?
   B: Yes, *it/there* is.
19 How long *does the journey take/takes the journey*?
20 How far *it is/is it*?

Correct the mistakes

2 There is one mistake underlined in each sentence. Note the mistakes and then write correct sentences.

1 A: What do you?
   B: I work in a factory.
   What do you do?

2 The restaurant closes on midnight.
....

3 She always goes to home at 5.30 p.m.
....

4 A: Why does he go to work by car?
   B: Because that he likes driving.
....

5 He travels never by underground.
....

Complete the conversation

3 Complete the conversation using the correct words.

A: Where ¹......*do*...... you work?
B: I ²................. in a library in ³................. city centre.
A: Is ⁴................. a good library?
B: Yes, ⁵................. is.
A: How ⁶................. is it ⁷................. the library from here?
B: About a mile.
A: Is it open ⁸................. Saturday?
B: Yes, it's open ⁹................. 9.30 a.m. ¹⁰................. 4 p.m.

CHECK YOUR PROGRESS
Look back at your answers for Units 11–15. Note your problem exercises and revise them.

UNITS 16–20

Shopping/prices

One/ones

2 Write questions and answers about the things in the shop, following the example.

1 CUSTOMER: *Could I have* .... two
   boxes of tissues, *please?*
   ASSISTANT: *The small ones or the*
   large ones?
   CUSTOMER: (D) *The large ones, please*

2 CUSTOMER: .... a
   notebook, ...
   ASSISTANT: ....
   ....
   CUSTOMER: (G) ....

3 CUSTOMER: .... four
   packets of crisps, ...
   ASSISTANT: ....
   ....
   CUSTOMER: (I) ....

4 CUSTOMER: .... a box
   of chocolates, ...
   ASSISTANT: ....
   ....
   CUSTOMER: (B) ....

1 Write questions about the prices of things in the shop.

1 (E) *How much are these envelopes?*
   They're 60p.

2 (G) ....
   It's 40p.

3 (B) *How much is that box of chocolates?*
   It's £6.00.

4 (H) ....
   They're 75p.

5 (I) ....
   They're 30p.

6 (C) ....
   They're 79p.

7 (F) ....
   It's £1.80.

UNIT 17

Countable and uncountable nouns

Countable nouns		Uncountable nouns
Singular	**Plural**	
a potato a loaf (of bread)	(some) potatoes	(some) bread (some) butter

3 Look at the picture and write sentences, saying where things are in the kitchen.

1 (coffee) *There is some coffee on the table.*

2 (milk) ....
.... *in the fridge*

3 (banana) ....
....

4 (biscuits) ....
....

5 (chicken) ....
....

6 (butter) ....
....

7 (mugs) ....
....

8 (purse) ....
....

Some and *any*

Positive	I've got some coffee/biscuits.
Question	Have you got any coffee/biscuits?
Negative	I haven't got any coffee/biscuits.

4 Look at the picture again. Complete the dialogue using *have got* and *some/any*.

A: 1 *Have you got any*
....
apples and oranges?

B: 2 *I've got some apples but I haven't got any oranges.*

A: 3 ....
salt and pepper?

B: 4 ....
....

A: 5 ....
eggs and bacon?

B: 6 ....
....

A: 7 ....
milk and sugar?

B: 8 ....
....

A: 9 ....
bread and butter?

B: 10 ....
....

Asking a friend to do some shopping

5 **Complete the conversation.**

A: Are you ¹ *going* to the shops?

B: Yes, I ²................ . Why?

A: Because we ³................ some milk.
⁴................ you get some?

B: OK. Anything ⁵................ ?

A: Well, we haven't got ⁶................ sugar. Have
⁷................ got ⁸................ money?

B: Yes, I ⁹................ Bye. See ¹⁰................ soon.

UNIT 18

Prepositions of place

6 **Complete the sentences about the two pictures, using the correct preposition.**

> on the corner of   between   opposite   in (x2)   behind (x2)   next to (x2)
> on the right of (x2)   in front of (x2)

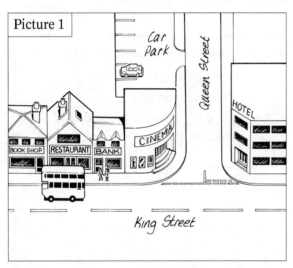

Picture 1

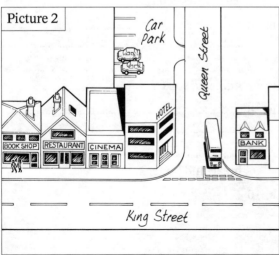

Picture 2

1 In Picture 1 the car park is ...... *behind* ......
the cinema, but in Picture 2 it is
behind .... the hotel.

2 In Picture 1 the bank is ....
the restaurant and the cinema, but in
Picture 2 it is .... the hotel
.... King Street and Queen
Street.

3 In Picture 1 the bus is ....
the restaurant ....
King Street, but in Picture 2 it is
.... the bank
.... Queen Street.

4 In Picture 1 the restaurant is ....
.... the bank, but in Picture 2 it is
.... the cinema.

5 In Picture 1 the cinema is ....
.... the bank, but in
Picture 2 it is .... the
restaurant.

Asking where places are

7 Put the sentences a)-g) in the correct order to make a conversation.

A

a) Oh good. I like curries. Thank you.

b) How far is Queen Street from here?

c) Excuse me, where's the car park?

d) Oh, that's not far. And is there a restaurant near the car park?

B

e) About one kilometre.

f) It's in Queen Street behind the hotel.

g) Yes, there's an Indian one in King Street next to the cinema.

1 C   2 ☐   3 ☐   4 ☐   5 ☐   6 ☐   7 ☐

Is Speaker A in the town in Picture 1 or Picture 2?
Speaker A is in the town in Picture ....

UNIT 19

Verb: *to be* (Past simple)

Positive	
It was	good.
They were	

Negative	
It wasn't	good.
They weren't	

Question		
What	was the weather	like?
	were the hotels	

Was it	good?
Were they	

Short answers			
Yes,	it was.	No,	it wasn't.
	they were.		they weren't.

8 Write questions and answers, using *What... like?* and the past simple.

1 A: (the weather)
   What was the weather like?
   B: (warm and sunny)
   It was warm and sunny.

2 A: (the nights)
   ....
   B: (very cold)
   ....

3 A: (your hotel)
   ....
   B: (small and friendly)
   ....

4 A: (the people)
   ....
   B: (kind and polite)
   ....

5 A: (the food)
   ....
   B: (very good)
   ....

9 Look at the notes. Write questions and short answers, using *was* or *were*.

> Our hotel
> Location - opposite the beach
> beautiful hotel gardens
> Bedrooms - small clean
> Restaurant - polite waiters boring food cold coffee

1 (hotel/near the beach)
Was the hotel near the beach?
Yes, it was.

2 (hotel gardens/lovely)
....
....

3 (bedrooms/big)
....
....

4 (bedrooms/clean)
....
....

5 (waiters/polite)
....
....

6 (restaurant food/interesting)
....
....

7 (coffee/hot)
....
....

Mixed tense revision

10 Look at the telephone conversation. Write the verbs in the correct tense.

A: Hello, Pam. How (be) [1] ...... *are* .... you?

B: I (be) [2] .... fine, thanks. The weather (be) [3] .... wonderful here! It (be) [4] .... very warm and the sun (shine) [5] ....

A: Oh! It (snow) [6] .... here at the moment. I (not like) [7] .... January in England! What (be) [8] .... your hotel like in Melbourne?

B: Wonderful! It (have got) [9] .... three swimming pools and four very good restaurants. Last week, there (be) [10] .... two parties in the hotel and last night there (be) [11] .... a barbecue on the beach. I (have) [12] .... a marvellous time here.

30

UNIT 20

Past simple

Positive	Negative
He went to America.	He didn't go to America.

Question	Short answers
Where did he go?	Yes, he did.
Did he go to America?	No, he didn't.

11 Complete the text with the past simple tense.

Last weekend we (go) ¹..*went*.. to Edinburgh by train from London. We (stay)²................. at a hotel in Princes Street. It (be) ³................. cold and windy when we (arrive) ⁴................. in Scotland, but the hotel (be) ⁵................. warm and comfortable. On Saturday morning, we (get up) ⁶................. at 8 o'clock and (have) ⁷................. a good breakfast. Then, we (walk) ⁸................. down Princes Street and (look) ⁹................. at the lovely shops. We (visit) ¹⁰................. the castle in the afternoon and (enjoy) ¹¹................. sitting in the gardens. We (not go) ¹²................. out in the evening, but we (stay) ¹³................. in the hotel and (talk) ¹⁴................. to some people from America.

12 Look at Exercise 11 again. Write short answers for these questions.

1 Did they go to Glasgow last weekend?
No, they didn't.

2 Did they go to Scotland by train?
....

3 Was it foggy when they arrived?
....

4 Was the hotel warm?
....

5 Did they like the shops in Princes Street?
....

6 Did they go out in the evening?
....

7 Were there some American people at the hotel?
....

13 Write questions about the text in Exercise 11, using the correct question word and the past simple of these verbs:

get up be travel stay go spend meet

1 *Where did they go*................. last weekend?
To Edinburgh.

2 ....
By train.

3 ....
Cold and windy.

4 ....
In a hotel.

5 .... on Saturday morning?
At 8 o'clock.

6 .... the afternoon?
At the castle.

7 .... in the evening?
Some American guests.

31

CHECK UNITS 16–20

Choose the correct answer

1 Circle the correct answer.

1 It *wasn't*/*weren't* cold yesterday.

2 The school is on *left*/*the left* of the car park.

3 A: How much is this?
B: *It*/*This* is £3.

4 I'd like *a*/*the* small ones, please.

5 Can I *help*/*helping* you?

6 How much are *any*/*the* envelopes?

7 A: Did they enjoy it?
B: Yes, they *enjoyed*/*did*.

8 I saw him *in front*/*in front of* the cinema.

9 A: Would you like a small coffee?
B: No, *I*/*I'd* like a large one, please.

10 Where did they *went*/*go* last night?

11 He is standing *next*/*next to* his sister.

12 We *have*/*haven't* got any biscuits.

13 There *are*/*is* some milk here.

14 The bank is on *the corner*/*corner* of North Street and London Road.

15 We need *a*/*some* bread.

16 *What*/*How* was your holiday like?

17 There is *some*/*any* bread here.

18 I didn't *travel*/*travelled* by bus.

19 How much *are*/*is* these pens?

20 Is *it*/*there* a bank near here?

Correct the mistakes

2 There is one mistake underlined in each sentence. Note the mistakes and then write correct sentences.

1 What the weather was like?
What was the weather like?

2 A: Are you going to the shop?
B: Yes, I go.
....

3 I live opposite to the park.
....

4 We having a wonderful time here.
....

5 A: Can I have a pen please?
B: A blue or a black ones?
....

Complete the story

3 Complete the story with the correct words.

Yesterday, Tracy ¹ *went*. by bus to visit a friend
² .... the country. She arrived ³ ....
11 o'clock. It ⁴ .... to rain and Tracy hadn't
⁵ .... an umbrella.

TRACY: Excuse ⁶ .... , are there ⁷ ....
shops near here? I need an umbrella.

MAN: Yes, ⁸ .... 's a little shop ⁹ ....
the corner. It ¹⁰ .... umbrellas.

TRACY: Thank you very much.

> **CHECK YOUR PROGRESS**
> Look back at your answers for Units 16–20.
> Note your problem exercises and revise them.

Question word: *Whose?*

1 Look at the pictures and write questions using *whose* and the correct form of *to be*.

1 <u>*Whose T-shirts are these?*</u>
They're Richard Booker's.

2 ....
They're Lucy Taylor's.

3 .... this?
It's Maggie Lee's.

4 ....
It's Jason's.

5 ....
They're Matthew Tucker's.

6 ....
They're Elizabeth Lacy's.

7 ....
It's Tom Stone's.

Belong to

2 Look at the pictures again. Write sentences using the correct form of the verb *belong to*.

1 (book)
<u>*The book belongs to Maggie Lee.*</u>

2 (pencils)
....

3 (car)
....

4 (T-shirts)
....

5 (keys)
....

6 (letters)
....

Possessive pronouns

Subject pronouns	Possessive adjectives	Possessive pronouns
I	my	mine
you	your	yours
he	his	his
she	her	hers
it	its	its
we	our	ours
they	their	theirs

3 Rewrite the sentences using possessive pronouns.

1 The pencils are Elizabeth's.
   The pencils are hers.

2 The notebook belongs to me.
   ....

3 The pen belongs to you.
   ....

4 The car is Tom's.
   ....

5 The house belongs to Mr and Mrs Lee.
   ....

6 The photographs belong to you and me.
   ....

7 The T-shirts belong to you and your sister.
   ....

4 Complete the questions and answers with the correct words.

1 A: Whose is this address book? Is it Tom's?
   B: No, it isn't ¹..... *his* .... . It belongs to me. It's
      ²............

   A: Whose diary is this? Is it yours?
   B: No, it isn't ³............. . It belongs to Tom. It's
      ⁴............. old diary.

2 A: Has Sue got a stereo system?
   B: Yes, this is ⁵............. . She got ⁶............. last
      week.
   A: Do the compact discs belong to Sue and
      Jason?
   B: Yes, they're ⁷............. . All these compact
      discs belong to ⁸............

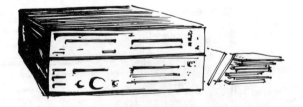

3 A: Does this dog belong to you and ⁹.............
      sister?
   B: Yes, it's ¹⁰............. dog. It belongs to
      ¹¹............. both.
   A: What does it want?
   B: It wants ¹²............. dinner.

UNIT 22

Adjective order

	plain	Colour	Pattern	
a	plain	dark green		skirt
		red and black	striped	

5 **Write the words in the correct order.**

1 │ and │ red │ a │ dress │ yellow │ flowery │

a red and yellow flowery dress

2 │ jacket │ bright red │ a │ checked │ blue │ and │

....

3 │ shirt │ an │ black │ and │ orange │ striped │

....

4 │ light │ blue │ a │ sweater │ plain │

....

5 │ green │ white │ a │ and │ patterned │ T-shirt │

....

Mixed tense revision

6 **Complete texts a)-c) with the correct forms of the verbs and then match them to pictures 1-3.**

| ride | hate | work | go (x2) | leave | study |
| wear | have | buy | can |

a) After Helen ¹....*left*........ school last summer, she ²................................. a long holiday. Now she ³................................. engineering at university and she ⁴... hard. [Picture ....]

b) In her free time, Helen ⁵................................. riding. She ⁶................................. a black horse called Prince. She ⁷................................. ride very well. [Picture ....]

c) Helen always ⁸................................. cheerful colours. She ⁹................................. colours like black, brown and dark green. Yesterday she ¹⁰................................. shopping and she ¹¹................................. a bright yellow patterned sweater. [Picture ....]

UNIT 23

Future: *going to*

Positive			Negative	
I'm	going to watch TV.		I'm not	going to watch TV.
She's			She isn't	
They're			They aren't	

Question						Short answers				
What	are you	going to do?		Are you	going to watch TV?	Yes,	I am.	No,	I'm not.
	is she			Is she			she is.		she isn't.
	are they			Are they			they are.		they aren't.

7 **Write questions, using *going to* and the following verbs:**

get come do wear buy stay have

BOB: 1 *What are you going to do* at the weekend, Sue?

SUE: I'm going to stay at Pete's house.

BOB: 2 .... there?

SUE: Because he's going to have a birthday party.

BOB: 3 .... his party?

SUE: At his parents' home. It's a big house in Rowlands Avenue in Bristol.

BOB: 4 .... there?

SUE: By train.

BOB: 5 .... at the party?

SUE: My new jeans and a red sweater.

BOB: 6 .... Pete for his birthday?

SUE: A watch.

BOB: 7 .... home?

SUE: On Monday morning.

8 **Look at the information in Exercise 7 and write short answers to these questions.**

1 Is Sue going to be at home this weekend?
   No, she isn't. ....

2 Is Pete going to have a birthday party this weekend?
   ....

3 Is his party going to be in Bristol?
   ....

4 Is his party going to be at a hotel?
   ....

5 Is Sue going to drive to Pete's house?
   ....

6 Is she going to wear casual clothes at the party?
   ....

7 Is she going to come home on Sunday evening?
   ....

Making suggestions

Making suggestions	Agreeing	Disagreeing
What about buying Pete a camera? Let's buy Pete a camera.	That's a good idea.	No, he's got one.

9 Complete the conversation.

CHRIS: What ¹ *are* we going to get Pete for ²............. birthday?

JANET: What about ³............. him some money?

CHRIS: No, it's his eighteenth birthday. ⁴............. buy him a present.

JANET: Yes, alright. What ⁵............. buying ⁶............. an alarm clock? ⁷............. always gets up late.

CHRIS: OK. ⁸............. do that.

Time adverbials

10 Complete the sentences with the following time adverbials:

> this evening
> next summer   at the weekend
> tomorrow   next week
> after our morning lesson

1 A: What are you going to do ...... *at the weekend* .....?

   B: I'm going to visit my parents.

2 I'm going to have a month's holiday in France ....

3 I was late for work today. I'm going to get up early ....

4 I'm going to walk to work every day ....

5 Let's have lunch in that new Chinese restaurant ....

6 A: What are you going to do ....

   B: I'm going to stay at home and watch a video.

UNIT 24

Describing people

11 Match the questions and answers.

a) They're brown.   e) He's very kind.

b) It's brown.   f) Yes, he does.

c) They're large red ones. g) He's very tall.

d) No, it's straight.

1 What's he like?
   e) He's very kind.

2 What does he look like?
   ....

3 What colour is his hair?
   ....

4 Is his hair curly?
   ....

5 What colour are his eyes?
   ....

6 Does he wear glasses?
   ....

7 What are his glasses like?
   ....

UNIT 25

Past simple

12 **Complete the story with the past simple forms of the verbs in brackets.**

I (watch) [1] _watched_ a long film on television
last night and it (be) [2] .... very late
when I (go) [3] .... to bed. I (read)
[4] .... a book in bed because I (can)
[5] .... not go to sleep. I (fall)
[6] .... asleep at about 2 a.m. but I
(wake) [7] .... up suddenly at 3.30 a.m.
because I (hear) [8] .... a loud noise in
the kitchen. I (walk) [9] .... downstairs,
(open) [10] .... the kitchen door and I
(see) [11] .... the 'burglar' – our cat! I
(shout) [12] .... at it and it (run)
[13] .... away through the open kitchen
window.

13 **Look at the story again in Exercise 12. Write short answers and give the correct information when you answer 'No'.**

1 Did he go to bed early?
No, he didn't. He went to bed
very late

2 Was there a film on television last night?
....
....

3 Did he watch it?
....
....

4 Did he read a newspaper in bed last night?
....
....

5 Did he fall asleep before midnight last night?
....
....

6 Was there a loud noise in the kitchen about 3.30 a.m.?
....
....

7 Did his dog make the noise in the kitchen?
....
....

8 Was the kitchen window closed?
....
....

14 Look at the information. Write questions and answers about Karen's journey to France yesterday.

	✗	✓
1 wake up		
2 go		
3 read		
4 drink		
5 spend	English money	French money
6 buy		

1 YOU: *Did you wake up at six o'clock?*
  KAREN: *No, I didn't. I woke up at eight o'clock.*

2 YOU: ....
  KAREN: ....
  ....

3 YOU: ....
  on the boat?
  KAREN: ....
  ....

4 YOU: ....
  in a French café?
  KAREN: ....
  ....

5 YOU: ....
  on the boat?
  KAREN: ....
  ....

6 YOU: ....
  KAREN: ....
  ....

Time adverbials

15 Complete the sentences, using the words in the boxes in the correct places.

1 | tomorrow   last week   yesterday |

Last week .... Sue went on holiday to America. I had a postcard from her .... She's going to visit Disneyland ....

2 | after lunch   in the morning
in the evening |

We're going to get up early .... because we're going to go shopping in town. At 2 p.m., ... , we're going to see a film. .... we're going to have dinner in a restaurant.

3 | in the afternoon   the next day
in the morning |

The little girl ate three ice creams .... before her lunch. Two hours later, ..., she had a box of chocolates. .... she was ill.

CHECK UNITS 21–25

Choose the correct answer

1 Circle the correct answer.

1 After *breakfast*/*the breakfast*, she went to school.

2 This bag is my *sisters*/*sister's*.

3 A: Whose book is this?
B: It's *her*/*hers*.

4 Let's *having*/*have* a party.

5 I like colours which *are looking*/*look* cheerful.

6 A: Is he going home now?
B: Yes, *he is*/*he's going*.

7 We're going to Paris *at*/*at the* weekend.

8 Whose *is*/*are* these jeans?

9 A: *What's he like?*/*What does he look like*?
B: He's very nice and friendly.

10 Are you going *to have*/*have* lunch now?

11 How much do you spend *for*/*on* clothes?

12 This *belongs*/*is belonging* to us.

13 The dog is having *its*/*it's* dinner.

14 You always get *very late to work*/*to work very late*.

15 Last night, she *read*/*reads* a good book.

16 What about *going*/*to go* to the cinema this evening?

17 She's got short dark *hair*/*hairs*.

18 I tried to telephone him yesterday, but I *couldn't*/*can't*.

19 I'm going shopping *and then*/*after* I'm going home.

20 *Was*/*Were* you at school yesterday?

Correct the mistakes

2 There is one mistake underlined in each sentence. Note the mistakes and then write correct sentences.

1 What you are going to do now?
What are you going to do now?

2 Whose this dog?
......

3 She is wearing a jacket black and yellow.
......

4 When I shouted, the man runned away.
......

5 This bag is mine, not their.
......

Complete the conversation

3 Complete the conversation with the correct words.

A: What ¹ *are* we going ² ...... do at ³ ...... weekend?

B: What ⁴ ...... going ⁵ ...... the theatre and ⁶ ...... having dinner ⁷ ...... that new Italian restaurant ⁸ ...... Princess Street?

A: That's ⁹ ...... good idea! Let's ¹⁰ ...... that.

CHECK YOUR PROGRESS
Look back at your answers for Units 21–25. Note your problem exercises and revise them.

UNITS 26–30

UNIT 26

Present continuous (Future use)

JULY

Sun.	**1**	*Carol - fly to Florida*
Mon.	**2**	*10.30 dentist*
Tues.	**3**	*7 a.m. children leave for camping holiday*
Wed.	**4**	*8 p.m. Harry's party at The Royal Hotel*
Thurs.	**5**	*Paul - take car to garage*
Fri.	**6**	*7 p.m. theatre with Pete and Jane*
Sat.	**7**	*10 a.m. tennis with Liz*

1 Look at Sue's calendar for next week (July 1st–7th). Complete the questions and answers.

1 *What's* Carol *doing* next Sunday?
She's flying to Florida.

2 When .... you .... to the dentist, Sue?
.... at 10.30 on Monday.

3 .... time .... the children .... for their holiday?
....
....

4 Where .... Harry .... his party?
....
....

5 What .... Paul .... on Thursday?
....

6 What .... Pete and Jane .... on Friday?
....

7 Who .... you ....
on Saturday, Sue?
.... with Liz.

2 Look at the information in the calendar. Answer the questions with short answers.

1 Is Sue going to the dentist on Monday afternoon?
No, she isn't.

2 Is Carol going to the USA on July 1st?
....

3 Are the children having a holiday in July?
....

4 Is Harry having a party on Thursday?
....

5 Are Pete and Jane going to the cinema on Friday?
....

6 Are Liz and Sue playing tennis on Saturday?
....

Adverbials and prepositions

3 Complete the text, using the following prepositions:

| at (x3) | on (x3) | to (x3) | in (x2) |
| from | after | before | |

Carol is flying [1] *to* Florida [2]............. Sunday morning. She is flying [3]............. Heathrow Airport [4]............. 10 o'clock [5]............. the morning. [6]............. she leaves, she is going [7]............. the bank to get some American dollars. She is staying [8]............. a big hotel [9]............. Florida. [10]............. 3rd July, she is meeting her American penfriend and they are going [11]............. a big Independence Day party [12]............. July 4th. [13]............. that, Carol is staying [14]............. her penfriend's house for three weeks.

41

Invitations

4 Put the sentences a)–h) in the correct order to make a conversation.

A

> a) Oh, I see. And what about Thursday. Are you working then?
> b) Are you very busy next week?
> c) Would you like to have Chinese, Indian or Italian food?
> d) Would you like to come for a meal with me next Wednesday or Thursday?

B

> e) Let's have Chinese.
> f) No, I'm not. That would be great.
> g) I'm quite busy. Why?
> h) Yes, I'd love to, but I can't on Wednesday. I'm working that evening.

1 [b] 2 [ ] 3 [ ] 4 [ ] 5 [ ] 6 [ ] 7 [ ] 8 [ ]

UNIT 27

Modal: *can* (request)

5 Make requests, using *Can I/you*.

1 (Ask a friend if you can use her phone)
   Can I use your phone, please?

2 (Ask someone if you can leave a message)
   ....

3 (Ask someone to phone you back tomorrow)
   ....

4 (Ask someone to help you)
   ....

5 (Ask a friend if you can drive her new car)
   ....

6 (Ask a friend to give John a message)
   ....

Modal: *will* (decision)

6 Make decisions for the situations (1–6) using *I'll* and the following verbs:

give help call take meet visit

1 You phone your friend's home. His mother tells you he is at his office.
   I'll call him there/at his office.............

2 Your friend tells you she is arriving at the airport at eight o'clock tomorrow.
   ....

3 You see an old lady trying to cross the road.
   ....

4 Your mother tells you your grandmother is in hospital.
   ....

5 Your friend says she hasn't any money for her train ticket.
   ....

6 You are trying on a coat in a clothes shop. You decide to buy it.
   ....

Talking on the telephone

7 Complete the telephone conversation.

ANNE: 69375. Hello.
PAUL: Hello, Anne. [1].......*It*.'s Paul [2]............ .
        [3].............. I speak [4].............. Tony, please?
ANNE: I'm [5].............., Tony's out [6].............. the
        moment. [7].............. I [8].............. a message?
TONY: Yes, [9].............. . Can you ask him
        [10].............. phone [11].............. this evening,
        please?
ANNE: Yes, I'll tell [12]..............
PAUL: Thanks. Goodbye.
ANNE: Bye for [13]..............

UNIT 28

Comparison of short adjectives

	Adjective	Comparative	Superlative
Regular adjectives	old big	older bigger	oldest biggest
Irregular adjectives	good bad	better worse	best worst

8 **Look at the information and complete the statements using comparative forms.**

Home | College

room: warm | small
food: good | cheap
friends: many | lively
life: easy | busy

1 My room at college *is smaller than my room at home.*

2 My room at home ....

3 Food at home ....

4 Food at college ....

5 I've got .... friends at home than at college.

6 My college friends .... my friends at home.

7 Life at home ....

8 Life at college ....

9 **Complete the statements with the superlative forms of the adjectives in brackets and these nouns:**

subject   child   city   month   day   time

1 (wet/dry) June was *the wettest month* and September was *the driest month* last year.

2 (good/bad) Science was my .... and music was my .... at school.

3 (old/young) Emma is my .... and Andrew is my ....

4 (early/late) Six o'clock is .... and nine o'clock is .... we can come.

5 (cold/hot) January 6th was .... and July 20th .... last year.

6 (pretty/ugly) Bath was .... and Birmingham was .... I visited in England.

UNIT 29

Comparison of longer adjectives

Adjective	beautiful
Comparative	more/less beautiful
Superlative	most/least beautiful

10 Look at the information and write sentences, using *more/less ... than.*

	+	–
1 interesting	golf	fishing
2 expensive	horse riding	tennis
3 boring	cricket	football
4 dangerous	boxing	football
5 enjoyable	tennis	fishing
6 difficult	tennis	table tennis

1 (interesting) I think fishing .... *is less interesting than golf*

2 (expensive) I think horse riding ....

3 (boring) I think football ....

4 (dangerous) I think football ....

5 (enjoyable) I think fishing ....

6 (difficult) I think tennis ....

11 Complete the sentences using words from the two boxes. Use superlative forms of the adjectives.

fashionable colour	in our family
famous building	in the zoo
amusing animals	in the house
dangerous room	in the city
interesting person	this winter
expensive hotel	in Paris

1 The kitchen *is the most dangerous room in the house.*

2 The Eiffel Tower ....

3 The Hilton ....

4 Dark blue ....

5 My uncle ....

6 The monkeys ....

UNIT 30

Present continuous and present simple

12 **The wrong verb forms are used in four of these sentences. Mark the sentences right (✓) or wrong (✗) and correct the wrong sentences.**

1 They like all sports. At the moment, they play tennis. (✗)
They like all sports. At the moment, they are playing tennis.

2 John is speaking four languages. He is speaking French now. (   )
....
....

3 Jane works at the airport. She likes her job very much. (   )
....
....

4 This morning, Mr Smith cleans his car and his son helps him. (   )
....
....

5 It rains a lot here in April, but the sun shines this morning. (   )
....
....

6 We usually live in New York, but this year we're living and working in London. (   )
....
....

13 **Write the correct forms of the verbs in brackets (present simple or present continuous).**

Tracy (be) ¹............*is*............ a student in London. She (come) ²........................ from Wales and her parents (live) ³........................ in Cardiff. This year, Tracy (live) ⁴........................ .... in a small student flat. At home in Cardiff, she (drive) ⁵........................ her mother's car, but at college she

(ride) ⁶........................ a bicycle. This weekend, Tracy's friend, Caroline, (visit) ⁷........................ her. Caroline (work) ⁸........................ in Cardiff. At the moment, Tracy (cook) ⁹........................ spaghetti bolognese and Caroline (make) ¹⁰........................ some coffee. Tracy (like) ¹¹........................ cooking but Caroline (hate) ¹²........................ it!

Mixed tense revision

14 **Write Caroline's answers to these questions, using the correct verb forms and the words in brackets.**

1 Where did you go last weekend, Caroline?
   (visit Tracy/London)
   I visited Tracy in London

2 Where is Tracy living?
   (student flat/near her college)
   ....
   ....

3 What's her flat like?
   (small/comfortable/quite cold in the winter)
   ....
   ....

4 What's Tracy studying?
   (music/work hard at the moment for her exams)
   ....
   ....

5 How does she spend her spare time?
   (play volleyball)
   ....
   ....

6 Where is she spending the Christmas holidays?
   (go to Austria with me for a ski-ing holiday)
   ....
   ....

7 Can you both ski?
   (Tracy/learn/last year. I/learn/at the moment)
   ....
   ....

Punctuation

15 **Write the sentences, using the correct punctuation:**

> full stop (.)   hyphen (–)   question mark (?)
> apostrophe (')   CAPITAL letter   comma (,)

1 A: is this car yours
   B: no it isnt
   A: *Is this car yours?*
   B: ....

2 A: whose is this t shirt
   B: its mikes
   A: ....
   B: ....

3 next monday im going to sues party she lives in york
   ....
   ....

4 A: would you like to come to a show on may the twenty first
   B: im sorry i cant im meeting my sister in paris then
   A: ....
   ....
   B: ....
   ....

CHECK *UNITS 26–30*

Choose the correct answer

1 Circle the correct answer.

1 A: Are you leaving now?
   B: Yes, I *am/are*.

2 They're coming *at/on* August 26th.

3 He's the *best/better* friend I've got.

4 Listen! The phone *is ringing/rings*.

5 He's working *as/as a* receptionist.

6 What *are you doing/do you do* next Monday?

7 Hello. *It's/I'm* Sue speaking.

8 He's *visiting/visiting to* his friend.

9 They *are liking/like* Paris very much.

10 Tony is older *than/as* you.

11 Can I *leaving/leave* a message, please?

12 She's Italian. *She's coming/She comes* from Naples.

13 *I'll lend/I'm lending* you some money. Here it is.

14 She's *a/the* most intelligent student in the class.

15 My children *learn/are learning* to swim.

16 Could you tell *him/to him* to ring me, please?

17 Is Jason *at work this morning/this morning at work*?

18 I think cricket is *lesser/less* interesting than football.

19 *Would/Will* you like to come to my party?

20 He was *the tallest/tallest* boy in the class.

Correct the mistakes

2 There is one mistake underlined in each sentence. Note the mistakes and then write correct sentences.

1 Your house is <u>more big</u> than mine.
   Your house is bigger than mine.

2 Can I speak <u>with</u> Tom please?
   ....

3 A: Would you like to come to my party?
   B: Yes, I'd <u>love</u>.
   ....

4 Thank you <u>to invite</u> me to your party.
   ....

5 Christmas Day is December the <u>twenty-five</u>.
   ....

Complete the conversation

3 Complete the conversation with the correct words.

A: Hello. ¹......*It*...... 's Bill here.

B: Hello, Bill. How ².................. you?

A: Fine, ³.................. . Are you ⁴.................. anything tomorrow evening?

B: ⁵.................. , I'm not. ⁶..................?

A: Well, I've ⁷.................. two free tickets for the theatre. ⁸.................. you like ⁹.................. come?

B: That would ¹⁰.................. great. Thank you.

CHECK YOUR PROGRESS
Look back at your answers for Units 26–30. Note your problem exercises and revise them.

UNITS 31–35

Modals: *can/could* (request)

1 Make requests for the situations, using *can* or *could*.

1 (You'd like to see the menu)
Can / Could I see the menu, please?
....

2 (You'd like to sit near the window)
....
....

3 (You want a glass of water)
....
....

4 (You want the waiter to open a window)
....
....

5 (You want the waiter to bring you some more coffee)
....
....

6 (You'd like the bill)
....
....

7 (You want the waiter to telephone for a taxi)
....
....

8 (You want to speak to the restaurant manager)
....
....

Modals: *would like* (offer) and *will* (decision)

2 Write questions and answers, using *Would you like …?* and *I'll have …* .

a) HUSMOROM UPSO

b) GONEAR JICEU

c) FOEFEC

d) CIE RAMEC

e) PAPEL

f) SPICH

1 *Would you like* .... something to drink?
c) Yes, please. I'll have a cup of coffee.

2 .... some rice or potatoes?
....

3 .... a starter?
....

4 .... a cold drink?
....

5 .... some fruit?
....
....

6 .... a dessert?
....
....

Offering and requesting

3 Put the sentences a)–i) in the correct order to make a conversation.

A

a) Yes, madam. And any potatoes?
b) Thank you, madam.
c) Would you like any vegetables or salad with your steak?
d) Are you ready to order, madam?
e) A salad, yes. And what would you like to drink?

B

f) I'll have a salad, please.
g) Yes. I'd like tomato soup to start with, please, and then steak.
h) No, thank you. Only the steak and a salad.
i) I'd like a glass of red wine, please.

1 [d]   2 [ ]   3 [ ]   4 [ ]   5 [ ]   6 [ ]   7 [ ]   8 [ ]   9 [ ]

UNIT 32

Present perfect

Positive	
He has (He's)	just broken a glass.
They have (They've)	

Negative	
He hasn't	passed the examination.
They haven't	

Question		
What	has he	done?
	have they	

Has he	left?
Have they	

Short answers			
Yes,	he has.	No,	he hasn't.
	they have.		they haven't.

4 Write positive and negative sentences, using the words in brackets.

1 (break/cup/plate)
I _haven't broken a cup. I've broken a plate._

2 (eat/apple/orange)
She ....
....

3 (find/watch/ring)
They ....
....

4 (buy/jacket/anorak)
I ....
....

5 (lose/camera/wallet)
She ....
....

6 (sell/bed/sofa)
I ....
....

7 (come/by bus/by train)
We ....
....

49

5 **Write sentences about pictures 1–7 above, using the present perfect and *just*.**

1 (leave)
The bus has just left.

2 (close)
....

3 (finish)
The film ....

4 (drop)
....

5 (bring/the soup)
....

6 (take/the sausages)
....

7 (break)
The boys ....

6 **Look at the pictures again. Write questions using the words in brackets and short answers.**

Picture 1:

1 (the bus/leave)?
Has the bus left?
Yes, it has.

2 (the man/get on the bus)?
....
....

Picture 3:

3 (the film/just/start)?
....
....

4 (the film/just/finish)?
....
....

Picture 6:

5 (the dog/take the sausages)?
....
....

6 (the dog/eat the sausages)?
....
....

UNIT 33

Present perfect with *ever*

7 Write questions using *ever* and the present perfect, then find the correct words a)–g) to make an answer.

a) 'Swan Lake'   e) Kenya
b) 'Hamlet'   f) the violin
c) Concorde   g) a Mercedes
d) the Prime Minister

1 (you/be/Africa)
   Have you ever been to Africa?
   e) Yes, I have. I've been to Kenya.

2 (they/see a ballet)
   ....
   ....

3 (he/learn to play a musical instrument)
   ....
   ....

4 (you/fly in a plane)
   ....
   ....

5 (she/drive a car)
   ....
   ....

6 (they/read a Shakespeare play)
   ....
   ....

7 (you/meet a famous person)
   ....
   ....

Been

8 Look at the picture and answer the questions.

1 Have you ever been to Canada, Simon?
   Yes, I have. I've been to Montreal.

2 Has Simon ever been to France?
   Yes, he has. He's been

3 Has Simon ever been to Holland?
   ....

4 Have you ever been to Spain, Simon?
   ....

5 Have you ever been to India, Simon?
   ....

6 Has Simon ever been to Australia?
   ....

7 Have you ever been to Portugal, Simon?
   ....

Present perfect

9 Write questions and answers, using *How many times...?*

1 (Janet and David/go to India/2)
How many times have Janet and David been to India?
They've been to India twice.

2 (David/ride an elephant/0)
....
....
....

3 (Janet/drink champagne/3)
....
....
....

4 (Janet and David/go to Italy/1)
....
....
....

5 (Janet and David/sleep in a caravan/0)
....
....
....

6 (David/eat a Korean meal/3)
....
....
....

7 (Janet/win a competition/2)
....
....
....

8 (David/lose an umbrella/3)
....
....
....

Past simple and present perfect

10 Write conversations.

1 A: (win £1,000) *I've won £1,000.*
  B: Congratulations!
     (how) *How did you win it?*
  A: (in a lottery) *I won it in a lottery.*

2 A: (break my arm) ....
  B: Oh dear!
     (when) ....
  A: (last weekend) ....

3 A: (find a gold watch)
     ....
  B: Really?
     (where) ....
  A: (in the park) ....

4 A: (lose my address book)
     ....
  B: Oh dear!
     (when) ....
  A: (yesterday) ....

UNIT 34

Saying what's wrong and offering help

11 Complete the sentences, using the following phrases:

| I feel (x2)   I don't feel   I've got (x2) |
| I've hurt (x2) |

1 *I've got* .... a cold.

2 .... dizzy.

3 .... my back.

4 .... very well.

5 .... very hot.

6 .... my head.

7 .... a temperature.

12 Say what's wrong, using *I feel* or *I've got*, then offer help using the pictures as prompts.

1 ..... *I feel* ..... tired.
Would you like to lie down?

2 .... a headache.
....

3 .... a cough.
....

4 .... dizzy.
....

5 .... a sore throat .
....

6 .... ill.
....

1

2

3

4

5

6

Invitations

13 Follow the instructions in the boxes and write the dialogue.

A: Ask B if she would like to come to the cinema with you this evening.

Would you like to come to the cinema with me this evening?

B: Refuse politely and explain that you don't feel very well .

....
....

A: Ask what the matter is.

....

B: You've got a sore throat and a temperature.

....

A: Ask B if she is going to the doctor's.

....

B: You're not going to the doctor's, but you're going back to bed.

....
....

A: Say you hope she'll feel better soon and you'll phone again tomorrow.

....
....

53

UNIT 35

Have got to

Positive	
I've	got to do some work.
He's	

Question	
Have you	got to do some work?
Has he	

Short answers			
Yes,	I have.	No,	I haven't.
	he has.		he hasn't.

Your interview is with Mr Dixon, the manager, at 9 a.m. on Tuesday, March 7th. Please bring your certificates and two passport size photographs.

14 John has got to do a lot of things before his interview tomorrow. Read what he says and write sentences using *have got to* and the following verbs:

buy   clean   find   wash (x2)   get (x2)

1 My car is dirty.
   I've got to wash my car.

2 My shoes are dirty.
   ....

3 I haven't got any money.
   ....

4 I don't know where my certificates are.
   ....

5 My hair is dirty.
   ....

6 I haven't got any passport size photographs.
   ....

7 I haven't got a tie.
   ....

Short answers

15 Look at the information in Exercise 14 and write short answers.

1 Has John got an interview tomorrow?
   Yes, he has.

2 Has he got a new car?
   ....

3 Is his car clean at the moment?
   ....

4 Has he got to wash his car before tomorrow?
   ....

5 Is he going to wear a tie tomorrow?
   ....

6 Has he got to take his passport to the interview?
   ....

Infinitive of purpose

16 **Match the two parts and write sentences, using *have got to* and the infinitive of purpose.**

1 She/go to the bank
2 I/move to America
3 I/phone my sister
4 They/sell their car
5 He/go to the post office
6 We/get up early
7 I/write to my uncle

a) tell her my news
b) thank him for his present
c) pay for their holiday
d) work in our New York office
e) catch the 6 a.m. train
f) cash a cheque
g) buy some stamps

1 *f) She's got to go to the bank to cash a cheque.*

2 ....

3 ....

4 ....

5 ....

6 ....

7 ....

Short forms

17 **Rewrite the sentences using short forms.**

1 A: What is your name?
   B: I am Sue.
   A: *What's your name?*
   B: *I'm Sue.*

2 A: Who is that?
   B: I do not know.
   A: ....
   B: ....

3 There is my sister. She has not seen us.
   ....
   ....

4 We will have chicken kiev and we would like some white wine.
   ....
   ....

5 A: Let us go to the cinema.
   B: I am sorry, I cannot. I have got to work tonight.
   A: ....
   B: ....

6 He is late because he has been to see the doctor.
   ....
   ....

CHECK UNITS 31–35

Choose the correct answer

1 Circle the correct answer.

1 What's *(the)/a* matter?

2 I *feeling/ feel* tired.

3 I think *I'll/I* have an ice cream, please.

4 I'm going to the bank *for getting/to get* some money.

5 They've *broke/broken* the window.

6 *I'd/I* like an orange juice, please.

7 She went to the *chemists/chemist's* to buy some plasters.

8 Would you like *to sit/sit* down?

9 He's got *a/the* headache.

10 Have they *ever visited/visited ever* you?

11 *I/I've* never been to Kenya.

12 Can I have a *glass water /glass of water*, please?

13 He *has/is* got to get up early.

14 *I've/I* got to go to work.

15 A: Have you got to leave now?
B: Yes, I *got to/have*.

16 I hope *you're/you* better soon.

17 The children *has/have* just left.

18 A: Has she won a car?
B: Yes, *she has/she won*.

19 Look! *I've/I* cut my finger.

20 Waiter! Can I have *the/a* bill, please?

Correct the mistakes

2 There is one mistake underlined in each sentence. Note the mistakes and then write correct sentences.

1 A: Have you been to London?
B: Yes, I've been.
Have you been to London?
Yes, I have.

2 Could I to see the menu, please?
....

3 He's gone to Canada three times.
....

4 What would you to drink?
....

5 I'm sorry I haven't wrote before.
....

Complete the conversation

3 Complete the conversation with the correct words.

A: Have you ¹ *ever* been ²............... The Railway Museum ³............... York?

B: No, I ⁴...............

A: ⁵............... you like to come ⁶............... me on Saturday?

B: I'm afraid I ⁷............... . I've ⁸............... to take my parents ⁹............... the airport. They're flying ¹⁰............... Canada on Saturday morning.

> **CHECK YOUR PROGRESS**
> Look back at your answers for Units 31–35.
> Note your problem exercises and revise them.

UNITS 36-40

Too + adjective and comparison of adjectives

1 Say what is wrong, using the words in brackets, and ask for alternatives using the following adjectives:

short cheap difficult quiet big young early light

1 (coat/small)
  This *coat is too small* .... for me.
  Have you got *a bigger one?*

2 (trousers/long)
  These ....
  Have you got .... pair?

3 (room/noisy)
  My ....
  I'd like ....

4 (train/late)
  The 10.30 .... for me.
  Is there ....

5 (English class/easy)
  My .... for me.
  Can I go to ....

6 (colour/dark)
  This ....
  Have you got .... blue?

7 (style/old)
  This .... for me.
  I'd like a suit in .... style.

8 (shoes/expensive)
  These ....
  Can I have .... pair, please?

Shopping

2 **Complete the conversation.**

ASSISTANT: 1..... *Can* .... I help 2................?

CUSTOMER: Yes, please. I'm 3.................. for
  4.................. blue jacket.

ASSISTANT: 5..................size?

CUSTOMER: Size 14.

ASSISTANT: There 6.................. some blue jackets
  here.

CUSTOMER: Have you 7.................. this style
  8..................a darker 9..................?

ASSISTANT: Yes. Here you 10.................. . Would
  you 11.................. to 12.................. it on?

CUSTOMER: Yes, please. (*Tries the jacket on*)
  It's fine. I'll 13..................it.

UNIT 37

Adverbs

	Adjective	Adverb
Regular	quick easy	quickly easily
Irregular	good early	well early

3 Make adverbs from the adjectives in brackets. Then rewrite the sentences with the adverb in the correct place.

1 (happy) The children played in the park.
The children played happily in the park

2 (good) She can speak English.
....

3 (fast) He never drives his car.
....
....

4 (loud) Don't speak to the children.
....
....

5 (early) I've got to get home this evening.
....
....

6 (careful) Do your homework.
....

7 (immediate) He always answers my letters.
....
....

8 (punctual) She arrived at 9 a.m.
....
....

Imperative (positive and negative)

4 Write positive and negative imperatives with the same meaning. For the negative imperatives, use these adjectives:

| loud   quick   bad   late   rude   casual   fast |

	Positive	Negative
1 (drive/slow)	*Drive slowly!*	*Don't drive fast!*
2 (sing/good)		
3 (behave/polite)		
4 (speak/quiet)		
5 (dress/smart)		
6 (come/early)		
7 (eat/slow)		

UNIT 38

No + -ing

5 Look at the notices and write the rules.

1   2   3

4   5   6

1 *No smoking.* ....

2 ....

3 ....

4 ....

5 ....

6 ....

Modal: *must/mustn't*

6 Complete the rules for the English Language School, using *must* or *mustn't*.

> ### THE NEW ENGLISH LANGUAGE SCHOOL
> *We speak English all the time!*

1 The students ...*mustn't*... speak their own language.

2 They .... speak English in the lesson.

3 They .... smoke in the classrooms.

4 They .... do their homework every night.

5 They .... eat in the lesson.

6 They .... take drinks into the classrooms.

7 They .... be punctual.

8 They .... tell the teacher if the don't understand the lesson.

Modals: *must/can/can't*

7 Read the information for staff. Complete the sentences with *must, can* or *can't*.

> ### THE ROYAL HOTEL
> *~ Information for staff ~*
>
> ALWAYS wear your uniform and be polite.
>
> NEVER cash cheques for hotel guests.
>
> Do NOT have your meals in the hotel restaurant.
> (The staff restaurant is Room 113 – free meals for all staff.)
>
> Do NOT park your car in the hotel car park.
> (The staff car park is at the back of the hotel.)
>
> Get your FREE ticket for the hotel disco from Mr Jones.

1 You ...*can't*... park your car in the hotel car park.

2 You .... park in the car park at the back of the hotel.

3 You .... be polite.

4 You .... have free meals.

5 You .... wear a uniform.

6 You .... eat in the hotel restaurant.

7 You .... cash cheques for guests.

8 You .... have a free ticket for the hotel disco.

UNIT 39

Feel + adjective

8 Write sentences with *feel*, an adjective and the present perfect or *going to*.

1 (happy/win £100)
He *feels happy because he has won £100.*

2 (sad/lose her gold ring)
She ....
....

3 (excited/fly to America next week)
They ....
....

4 (frightened/just /watch a horror film)
I ....
....

5 (nervous/take an examination tomorrow)
He ....
....

6 (lonely/just /move to a new town)
She ....
....

When + present simple

9 Write questions or answers, following the example.

1 A: *How do you feel when your holiday ends?*
B: When my holiday ends, I feel sad.

2 A: What colour do you think of when you hear the word 'happy'?
B: ....
.... yellow.

3 A: ....
....
B: When I listen to the news, I usually feel depressed.

4 A: How do you feel when it's your birthday?
B: .... happy.

5 A: ....
....
B: When I lie in bed and listen to the rain, I feel safe.

6 A: How do you feel when you meet new people?
B: ....
.... nervous.

UNIT 40

To be born

10 Write questions and answers about where or when these people were born.

1 (Richard Wagner/Leipzig)
Where was Richard Wagner born? He was born in Leipzig.

2 (Sir Winston Churchill/1874)
....
....

3 (Abraham Lincoln/ Kentucky)
....
....

4 (Charles Darwin/1809)
....
....

5 (Mohandas Gandhi/1869)
....
....

6 (Napoleon Bonaparte/Corsica)
....
....

Past simple with *for* and *ago*

For			Ago		
He worked there	for	several months. three years.	He went there	several years three years	ago.

11 Look at the diagram, then answer the questions about Sandra, using *for* or *ago*.

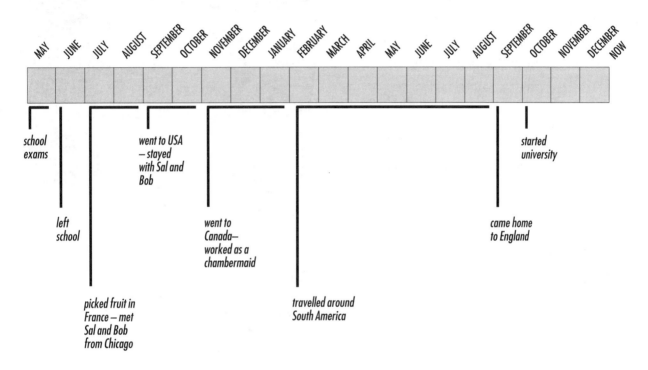

1 When did Sandra leave school?
She left school about eighteen months ago.

2 When did she first meet Sal and Bob?
....
....

3 How long did she pick fruit in France?
....
....

4 How long did she work in Canada?
....
....

5 When did she leave Canada?
....
....

6 How long did she travel in South America?
....
....

7 When did she come home from South America?
....
....

8 When did she start university?
....
....

61

After/before + -ing

12 Look at the information about Sandra in Exercise 11. Write sentences using the words in brackets, beginning *After/Before ... ing.*

1 (take exams/leave school) *After taking her exams, Sandra left school.*

2 (leave school/work in France) ....

3 (go to university/travel for a year) ....

4 (stay with Sal and Bob/go to Canada) ....

5 (return home/spend several months in South America) ....

6 (spend a month at home/begin her university studies) ....

Welcome to Peru

Canada

Prepositions

13 Complete the paragraph with the following prepositions:

ago (x3)	on (x2)	in (x6)	for (x2)	of

My grandmother was born 65 years ¹ *ago*
² .... May 6th. ³ .... 60 years, she
lived ⁴ .... the same town ⁵ .... the
north ⁶ .... England. Her son, my uncle
Will, went to live ⁷ .... America ⁸ ....
1980, and five years ⁹ .... my grandmother
moved to Boston to be near uncle Will and his
family. ¹⁰ .... May I'm going to visit them. I
haven't seen my uncle ¹¹ .... four years.
He came to England four years ¹² .... on
business. ¹³ .... May 6th, we're going to
have a big birthday party for my grandmother
¹⁴ .... Boston.

Punctuation

14 Punctuate the sentences.

1 sandra went to bristol university in october
Sandra went to Bristol University in October

2 sandras friends bob and sal live in chicago
....
....

3 its a lovely day isnt it lets go out
....
....

4 drive slowly that childs going to run across the road
....
....

5 my parents and i live at 16 king street in hull
....
....

CHECK UNITS 36–40

Choose the correct answer

1 Circle the correct answer.

1 This coat is too small.
   Have you got *bigger*/*a bigger* one?

2 *I*/*I'll* take this jacket, please.

3 Speak *quiet*/*quietly*!

4 You must *being*/*be* punctual.

5 She *left*/*has left* school a year ago.

6 Could I *try*/*to try* this on, please?

7 What *happens*/*is happening*?

8 You can't *smoke*/*smoking* in here.

9 After *go*/*going* to the bank, I did some shopping.

10 You *can*/*must* wait here if you want to.

11 Where *you*/*were you* born?

12 He feels very *happily*/*happy*.

13 They sing very *badly*/*bad*.

14 *Would*/*Do* you like to come to my party?

15 Always be *politely*/*polite*.

16 My birthday is *in*/*on* June 26th.

17 We *live*/*lived* there for several years.

18 She felt nervous before *to sing*/*singing*.

19 How do you feel when your holiday *ends*/*will end*?

20 I told them *a week*/*last week* ago.

Correct the mistakes

2 There is one mistake underlined in each sentence. Note the mistake and then write the correct sentences.

1 You <u>mustn't to park</u> here.
   You mustn't park here.

2 I <u>am born</u> in Madrid.
   ....

3 She <u>speaks very well German</u>.
   ....

4 Please <u>not to smoke</u>.
   ....

5 When I <u>waking up</u>, I feel happy.
   ....

Complete the conversation

3 Complete the conversation with the correct words.

A: Excuse ¹....*me*...., can ².................. leave my car ³.................. the street?

B: No, ⁴.................. afraid you ⁵.................. . One of the company rules ⁶.................. that you ⁷.................. always park ⁸.................. the company car park and never in ⁹.................. street.

A: OK. ¹⁰.................. do that. Thanks.

CHECK YOUR PROGRESS

Look back at your answers for Units 36–40. Note your problem exercises and revise them.

GRAMMAR INDEX

The numbers indicate the pages where each item can be found.